Chinatown, San Francisco

Photographs by Phil Palmer

Text by Jim Walls

HOWELL-NORTH

Portrait of a city within a city

SAN FRANCISCO'S CHINATOWN is the largest Oriental City in the Western Hemisphere. Flowering in the heart of a metropolis, on the northern edge of San Francisco's downtown, Chinatown remains a separate city, inside the larger city and yet out of it. Working and thriving, catering to throngs of tourists, the Chinese of Chinatown contemplate their separate past which brought each of them, later or sooner, across the gulf of the Pacific.

No matter where in the breadth of America the Chinese may have wandered, San Francisco is still their capital and the focus for their yearnings. It is a place where the festivals are properly observed, where the language is spoken with grace and written with flourish. Now especially when mainland China is closed to them, it is a place where America's Chinese can be buried amidst the graves of their kinfolk.

The fabled opium dens have vanished and the sound of moon viols no longer issues from the haunts of slave girls. Highbinders and hatchetmen no longer prowl the community's exotic corridors. Chinatown today lacks even juvenile delinquency to lend it an aura of violence, and the worst that can be said of it is that the festive click of dominoes occasionally enlivens a subterranean attempt at gambling (non-Chinese need not apply). And yet Chinatown still seems shadowed in mystery. Adventure seems to lie beyond doorways that lead suddenly, mysteriously downward into strangely lighted basements. The sense of mystery thickens in the narrow, dimly lighted alleys. Sometimes the feeling is justified. This doorway or that, unprepossessing as it fronts the street, will lead upward to one of the gilded meeting halls of the great associations—rich chambers filled with carvings and brocaded paintings.

Soo Yuen Tong Family Associaiton, Grant Avenue

One of many bars
whose Oriental atmosphere
pleases tourists.

Waverly Place, indulging a
small Chinese sweet tooth.

In San Francisco, one comes upon Chinatown suddenly, with a shock of surprise. It lies north of Bush Street, just beyond the world of high fashion. Or it spreads out west of Kearny, a block away from Montgomery Street, the so-called "Wall Street of the West." In the space of a breath, or so it seems, the furs and diamonds of the West are exchanged for the silk and jade of the East.

Chinatown's main street is Grant Avenue, once the main street of the whole of San Francisco. In "The Flower Drum Song," C. Y. Lee observed that "to the casual tourists, Grant Avenue is Chinatown, just another colorful street in San

Interior, food market

Grant Avenue scene

Sidewalk decoration

Francisco; to the overseas Chinese, Grant Avenue is their showcase, their livelihood; to the refugees from the mainland, Grant Avenue is Canton." Narrow and one way, Grant Avenue is as swarmingly alive as any Oriental street ever pictured. On bright days, the sun glints on its painted balconies, three and four floors above the crowds who almost never cross the street at the intersections. The air carries the incessant sound of Cantonese, the strident call of a new phonograph record from Formosa, the icy tinkle of glass bells.

For six blocks to the north of Bush Street, Grant Avenue mixes a devotion to tourists with some of the Nation's most elaborate Chinese restaurants, places patronized by both

Two views of Grant Avenue at night. Feelings are sharply divided as to whether the night or day is more glamorous in Chinatown.

Orientals and Occidentals. The sides of the street are lined with gift shops, jewelry stores and art goods houses, all of which manage to stay in stock despite the ban on imports from mainland China. Mixed with Chinese objects from Hongkong and Formosa, an infiltration of Japanese goods is reflected in some show windows. One ingenious proprietor, plainly a compulsive importer, now displays cigarettes from everywhere.

After two more blocks, Grant Avenue drifts out of Chinatown, fading into a Mexican barrera, a Little Manila, a colony of Basques and a large Italian section. But these last two blocks are, in a sense, "downtown" to the Chinese, for they provide at least an all-Chinese shopping center. They contain furniture and appliance shops, banks, grocery stores and meat markets. Facing the street, the food store windows are minor museum pieces, decorated with live fish swimming in display tanks, with live poultry strutting in street-

Grant Avenue gift, clothing shop.

10

side pens, with hanging strings of glazed ducks and with all the exotic vegetables that make up the Chinese menu.

This, the up-and-back round trip on Grant Avenue is as much of Chinatown as the casual tourist ever sees — just this one crowded street jammed with automobiles parked under "No Parking" signs, an exercise in Oriental fatalism which the police have, perhaps wisely, decided to ignore.

The whole of Chinatown includes five blocks of Stockton

Gift shop interior.

Sidewalk vendor.

To the left, a dry goods store. To the right a table of gifts and mementos.

A custom
seamstress.
She works at
one of the fine
silk houses.

Modeling a
dress at the
"City of Shanghai" shop.

15

Street, extended sections of the cross streets from Pine to Broadway and a complicated interlacing of alleys—Waverley Place, Pagoda Alley, Spofford, Wentworth, Duncombe, Ross Alley, Old Chinatown Lane—some gaudy with color, others dark and deceptively sinister. But it is in these places, away from Grant Avenue, that most of Chinatown's landmarks are to be discovered. Even Old St. Mary's, a fortress of devotion on a Grant Avenue corner, has a California Street address.

To the side of this former Roman Catholic cathedral, where the Paulist Fathers have conducted a mission to the Chinese since 1902, is a small park, St. Mary's Square, now the landscaped rooftop of an underground garage. A splatter of green trending downward toward Kearny, the square is presided over by a brooding, stainless steel statue of Sun Yat-sen, who plotted the destruction of the Manchu Empire in a room not three blocks distant. Also in Chinatown, or framed on three sides by it, is Portsmouth Square, the oldest in the city.

**Jackson Street from Grant Avenue.
San Francisco-Oakland Bay Bridge in background.**

The plaza of San Francisco's earliest days, when the city was a raw village, Portsmouth Square passed through its period of greatness surrounded by gaiety and gambling establishments. The center of today's city has swirled onward, leaving Portsmouth Square in a backwash almost of quiet. It is marked by a monument to Robert Louis Stevenson, who once found the square a pleasant place to sit. Today, many Chinese find it a pleasant place to sit, and Chinese children romp on its lawns.

California Street cable car climbs the hill. Old St. Mary's Church in the background.

Left, the statue of Dr. Sun Yat-sen, famous founder of the Chinese Nationalist Party, overlooks St. Mary's Square.

17

Chinatown Alleys

Left, Old Chinatown Lane, formerly Cameron Place. Chingwah Lee's museum is at far left. Semi-circular apertures at ground level are to light basements.

Spofford Street.

Below, Pagoda Alley.

Wentworth Place and Jackson Street.

As open places, these are few enough for Chinatown which has always been the most densely packed area in the city. Before the last war, the community averaged 20.4 persons per bath, 12.3 persons per kitchen. Since then, this density has been partly relieved by the construction of the Ping Yuen (or "peaceful garden") housing project on Pacific Street—three imposing structures built in semi-Chinese style.

It has also been relieved by the flow of Chinese through the Pacific Street pass between Nob Hill and Russian Hill, and their slow spread on the hills' farther sides. It might be said that Chinatown now extends as far as Polk Street, a mile to the west, although this postwar suburbia (to Grant Avenue's downtown) betrays few Oriental features other than its inhabitants. And yet it also has its little touches—a display of tropical fish in the window of a laundry, a wrought-iron entryway moulded in the form of Chinese writing.

Packed as the original Chinatown was, few Chinese wanted to leave it, and those on the other side of the hills figure that they haven't left it. The Grant Avenue area, after all, had been their city, almost their private city, for over a

**Playground at Portsmouth Square,
Hall of Justice in background.**

Portsmouth
Square

century. Indeed, from one point of view, it was two cities, one on top of the other, the split occurring horizontally somewhere in the neighborhood of the second floor. Below, at the edge of the street, was the city they still call *Sang Yee Gah,* the business city of shops and stores, a scene of noise and crowds. Above, rising in the air, was what is still called *Gee Gah,* the city where people live and where the great associations have their serene council chambers. *Gee Gah* is a city of sculpture and carvings, of hanging scrolls and embroidered paintings, of incense burning before the gods of the families and districts. It is a city of heavy, hand-carved, imported furniture. It is a quiet city, where the street noises are dim in the depths below. *Gee Gah* is undefiled China, transplanted to this Western shore.

And yet *Sang Yee Gah,* the commercial city, is fascinating partly because it *is* defiled by Western ways. Since *Sang Yee Gah* has made its compromises with the greater city that surrounds it, it is, in its way, unique in the world. Here, a statue of Buddha sits behind the open door of a shop and contemplates the other side of the street, where chalk marks announce that "Nancy Hong loves Larry Chen." A bearded elder slides through Grant Avenue in a convertible Jaguar. The sidewalk candy merchants stock all-day suckers and Tootsie Rolls. An old lady, definitely one who clings to the customs of a past era, makes her slow passage down the sidewalk. At a word she turns and smiles and accepts the arm of a Chinese dandy dressed in a Brooks Brothers suit.

Chan Family Association building.

Interior of Kong Chow Temple
on Pine Street. Oven-like structure
at rear is for burning paper prayers.

陳柳亭廬
潁川堂二樓查歸

ENG HUNG CHI
BEAN CAKE Cº.
132

Above—Name and location
of upstairs resident.

香亞街
HANG AH ST.
(PAGODA AL.)

CHINATOWN POST Nº 4618

遠征退伍軍人華埠分會

24

Chinatown's signs

Chinese herb shop window.

MANAGER'S OFFICE
Mr. Frank Lee
RM. 309

茶樓辦事處

李冷恩先生

評樓屋尽

醫　三樓三零三

者　李銘超

男婦全科

YAN NIN TONG & CO.
807

延年堂

Blending of cultures

*W*REATHED IN THE SHADOWS of the past are the legends —that the Chinese, who are certainly excellent mariners, crossed the broad Pacific in the ancient days and landed in California. Better established is the fact that there were seven Chinese in San Francisco *before* the Gold Rush, all recent arrivals, and one of these was a merchant, Chum Ming, a citizen of China's southernmost province, Kwangtung. When gold was discovered, Chum Ming headed for the hills and made a strike. He reported the good news, by letter, to Cheong Yum in Kwangtung, and tales of distant riches raced through the province like a wind-whipped prairie fire. By 1851, there were 12,000 Chinese men in California—and seven women.

At first, the Chinese were regarded as lovable and exotic curiosities, decorating San Francisco's parades and civic functions clad in silk pantaloons and wearing long, braided queues. But as a reservoir of cheap and untiring labor, the Chinese soon clashed with other laborers—first the miners, later the construction gangs on the Central Pacific railway. Reacting passively, seeking at all costs to avoid clashes with Americans, the Chinese were soon harried from every side— with discriminatory taxes, with threats, and in a few cases with massacres. They responded by organizing themselves into associations for mutual aid, associations which continue to this day to be a powerful force in Chinatown.

When the Central Pacific was completed in 1869, brigades of unemployed Chinese laborers turned to the land. They cleared forests, reclaimed swamps, threw up the massive dikes in the Delta country, planted and harvested the state's crops. But the spectre of cheap labor, aided by the financial crash of 1875, urged on the sandlot speakers (the

Mailboxes, Old Chinatown Lane.

Contemporary
Chinese porcelain.

sandlot was an open area west of Van Ness Avenue where crowds could be harangued without disturbing the peace) to issue their war cry, "The Chinese must go!" The result was that while the Chinese didn't go, more were prevented from coming into California by the exclusion acts, the first of which was passed in 1882. But by that time, there were already 75,000 Orientals in the state. One out of every seven Californians was Chinese.

And by this time, also, the associations which the Chinese had formed for mutual aid had produced a Frankenstein offspring, the warring tongs. The origin of these groups is obscure, some of them allegedly springing out of revolutionary organizations in China, but none of them ever behaved in China the way they misbehaved in San Francisco. They set the pattern for the Chicago gangsters of the Prohibition era.

On its seamier side, Chinatown was the scene of traffic in slave-girl prostitutes, in narcotics and in gambling—activities all controlled by one or another of the warring tongs. To maintain their power, the tongs resorted to blackmail, intimidation and assassination. Enemies were "put on the spot" and killed by hired gunmen, called "hatchetmen" or "highbinders." Tong leaders moved about in a convoy of body guards, and their most famous member, "Little Pete," was caught with his guard down, like the more recent Albert Anastasia, and bumped off while seated in a barber chair.

Three generations of one family.

The telephone exchange on Washington Street—replica of a small temple.

4000 subscribers chose to be reached by name, disregarded the telephone company's number system.

Other hundreds of Chinese were killed by highbinders before the Tong Wars finally ended, in 1926.

The protective clannishness of the Chinese gave rise to evil legends made all the more sinister by this atmosphere of vice. Chinatown was an interconnected catacomb, it was said, with basements going six floors underground where the blackest deeds were enacted. But the Chinatown that was flattened and destroyed by the firequake of 1906 revealed only the usual number of basements. There was much talk, at the time of the fire, of settling the Chinese elsewhere, but when the smoke cleared, they rushed right back to Grant Avenue and started to rebuild—any old way, anything for a shelter in their old home.

The traditional Chinese fondness for children is widely evident.

At this point, the telephone company rebuilt its CHina exchange, a prefix now extinct. The bilingual girl operators of the CHina exchange were eventually required to know the whereabouts of 4000 subscribers by name, for the Chinese rarely asked for a number. Their new building was a small jewel, a replica of a Chinese temple, set on Washington Street, where it still stands. This was the spark that Chinatown needed, and the community was rebuilt with an oriental look, for the most part. The exotic flavor was enhanced, in 1925, by the installation of the famed, twined-dragon street lights.

After the first World War, the Chinese of Chinatown cut off their

American police find no delinquency problem here.

queues, which they had come to regard as "reactionary" symbols of Manchu oppression. The new generation started discarding their Chinese clothing in favor of Western-style dress. Speaking the revered Chinese language came to be more a matter of preference than a command of the elders. Slowly, it became no longer necessary to bow to the elders before addressing them at any official gathering.

After World War II, the Americanization of this Oriental island in San Francisco's center proceeded at an ever quickening pace. Restrictive real estate covenants no longer bound the Chinese so tightly to the region around Grant Avenue. Job opportunities opened up, and the one-time "Chinaboy," who was thought good only for taking in washing or harvesting carrots, is now an engineer, a lawyer, an accountant, a scientist.

And yet San Francisco's Chinese—perhaps because their heritage is so rich and civilized—are far from abandoning all the old ways. Chinese remains the predominate language, and even the youngest children continue to understand it, if not to speak it among themselves. Chinatown has turned into a blend of cultures in which the East still predominates.

Sidewalk display of packaged tea, notions, candy.

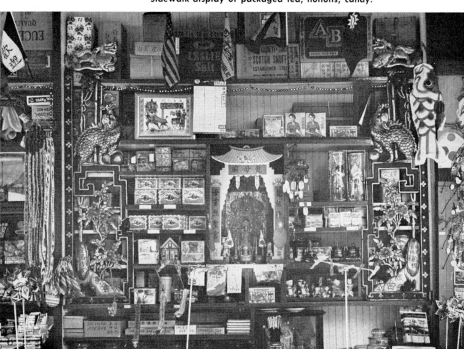

Ceremonial weapons.

"Li Sheng Kuan" incense urn
for Taoist deities.

Every day people gather to read the latest
news at the several Chinese newspapers.
This is the "Chinese World."

Fortune slips in a Chinese temple.

Silver pagoda.

Herb shop window.

Chingwah Lee Studio on Old Chinatown Lane.

34

Chinese art and decoration

Golden dolphin.

Below, mortuary earthenware in the Chingwah Lee Studio. It is dated from 3000 B.C. to 960 A.D.

The Associations

A VISITOR TO CHINATOWN, not so long ago, was asked to look at Coit Tower, atop Telegraph Hill. From his vantage point on Stockton Street, the visitor was asked by his guide, "Now, do you see the small temple on top of the Six Companies building?" The visitor noted a very small temple on the roof. Said the guide: "This is the story. When the great Chinese scholar, Fong Shew Louie, came here and saw the Coit Tower, he declared it interfered with the Six Companies location. Such a great tower, he said, interfered with the

Chinese Six Companies.

natural attraction the Six Companies had for the favor of heaven. He suggested that the Six Companies build a tower, and it was done.

"Now," added the guide, "look at the green building. Do you see the small green tower? That is the tower of the Hop Sing Association—you know, tong. It too was built to offset the power of the Coit Tower. The day after the Hop Sing tower was built, the president of the Hop Sing tong won $8000 at lottery."

This story is typical of San Francisco's Chinatown, where East is intertwined with West. It would seem strange to other San Franciscans that anything as powerful as the Six Companies would ever need the protection of a simple wooden tower.

For their mutual assistance in an alien land, San Francisco's Chinese banded together, soon after the Gold Rush, in a bewildering variety of associations. Yet when analyzed, the associations are seen to be of three main types.

Altar in the Sam Yup Family Association.

First are associations organized for a definite purpose. The purpose may be quite innocuous—such as seeking perfection on certain musical instruments, and Chinatown abounds in musical societies. Or the purpose might in earlier days have been more sinister—the so-called warring tongs thrived on and controlled gambling and prostitution.

More important are the family associations—the Chans, Wongs, the Four Families and a score more—made up of people who bear the same name. Presided over by a council, each family organization looks after the welfare of its members, and its influence extends across the continent.

On Ping Family Association.

At their last San Francisco convention, for example, the Wongs attracted 10,000 other Wongs from all corners of the United States.

Finally, there are the district associations, each of whose members come, personally or by ancestry, from the same district in the Chinese province of Kwangtung. Almost all of San Francisco's Chinese have their origins in seven

37

Where else are snakes
and dragons so easy
to acquire?

districts, and the seven district associations make up the Six Companies (so-called because at one time it was composed of only six district associations).

In recent years, the Chinese have come to use American courts as the places to settle grievances, but for many years they didn't. (It was said that a Chinaman's oath was worthless, since he was a heathen, and therefore his testimony couldn't be trusted.) In earlier days, the Six Companies were the ultimate tribunal in Chinatown, and from Six Companies' decisions, there was no appeal. It was a government within a government, ruling at one time a sizable part of the population of California. A mysterious organization in Western eyes, the Six Companies were the source of dark legends and every evil was attributed to them. But their greatest evil, as history now shows, was that the Six Companies worked exclusively for the welfare of the Chinese.

Today, Six Companies functions have become largely ceremonial. Yet their prestige remains high in Chinatown, and they continue to operate in their imposing Stockton street headquarters protected against the power of Coit Tower by their own rooftop temple.

38

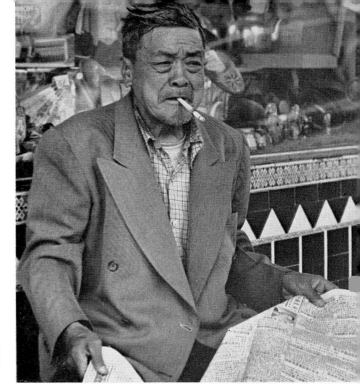

There are five
Chinese newspapers
well supported
by the population.

A Chinese calligrapher.
See abacus to the left of picture.

The children

The beautiful silks and rich brocades available
in Chinatown have proved a great source
of inspiration to the coutourier.
Western evening clothes and cocktail
dresses have gained distinction from a touch
of the Oriental. Visitors to San Francisco
highly prize a custom made garment
as a memento of Chinatown.
For those who can't indulge in this
luxury, there are many ready-made clothes
in all price ranges.

Modern mother and pony-tailed
daughter along Grant Avenue.

Some beautiful Chinese girls in modern adaptation of Chinese dress, or modeling traditional costumes.

The ancient tongue endures

IN THE DAYS WHEN SAN FRANCISCO was scourged by high-binders, four murderers were sentenced to hang, and all, according to the daily *Alta California,* spent their final hours composing poetry. One of them, for example, wrote:

> My body hath gone before me, borne on clouds.
> My youth was coupled with twenty springs.
> I was unconscious of it, but thus it was.
> I loved to follow the bridegroom of the Southern Hills.

When the Chinese came to America, they brought with them their heritage, China, and they wrapped themselves in it as in a cocoon. Beyond a passion for poetry which found expression even among hoodlums, this heritage contained the most precious thing of all—the ancient expressive Chinese language.

There are, to be sure, many Chinese languages, especially south of the Yangtze river where archaic forms have been preserved. In the remote south of Kwangtung province, the old home of San Francisco's Chinese, one farmer will have difficulty understanding another who lives as little as 50 miles away. In San Francisco, the Chinese are said to speak Cantonese, and many of them do speak the dialect of the city of Canton. Most of them, however, do not. The ancestors of these came from the farm lands outside the city, and they understand the speech of Canton only by straining their ears.

Speakers of Peking dialect, the so-called Mandarin which has been elevated to the national language of China, have sneered at San Francisco speech as the prattle of hicks. But for all its country overtones, the local Chinese language is written in exactly the same way as Mandarin, and the great written classics of Chinese civilization are as readily available in Chinatown as they are (or perhaps were) in Peking.

All Chinese children attend special schools each afternoon when public schools have finished. Here they are taught the Chinese language, history, geography, art and calligraphy.

Abacus. This size will compute to 100,000,000. The Chinese calculate on these with amazing speed. It permits addition, subtraction and multiplication.

Proud of their heritage and determined to protect it, the local Chinese have set up a number of Chinese language schools which their children attend each day after they have attended a regular American grammar school. Seemingly out of nowhere, swarms of shouting, laughing Chinese children suddenly appear in the streets of Chinatown each weekday evening about 5 o'clock. They have just been dismissed from their classes in Chinese language and calligraphy, and they carry simplified copies of the classics under their arms.

Almost all business among the inhabitants of Chinatown is still conducted in the Chinese language, and its use on ceremonial occasions is absolutely required. A stylish mastery of the Chinese language remains essential for advancement within the tight hierarchy of Chinese society. The ultra-sophisticated Chinese will blend Chinese and English, using whichever portrays a given sentiment most expressively.

Members of the latest generation, the first to be offered great opportunities in the larger American scene, are less immersed in the Chinese way of life than their parents were. The Chinese opera is no longer attended often enough for regular performances, and its elaborate costumes continue to be brought out only on rare occasions. The temples now hold combined services for Buddhists, Confucianists and

At right, Kuan Yin,
Goddess of Mercy,
in the Buddist Temple.

Children play
Chinese game in
doorway.

Taoists because the congregations, mostly elders, are no longer large enough to support separate temples for the three faiths—except for a recent upsurge in Zen Buddhism, and with it a new Zen Temple by the side of Portsmouth Square. Most of San Francisco's Chinese are by now Christians.

And yet Chinatown continues to act as a preservative of Chinese culture in America. A local Chinese scholar expressed it this way: "Any one who doesn't like the Chinese atmosphere of Chinatown will move elsewhere—to some place like Iowa where he can become completely Americanized and absorbed into the general culture. The Chinese who do like the Chinese atmosphere tend to stay here, or to come back from distant places. It is not unusual for a successful Chinese businessman in some place like Montana to sell his business, when he has enough money, and return to San Francisco where his children can learn the Chinese language."

Though no longer presented regularly, the opera
still boasts elaborate costumes and scenery.

Three members of the cast pose informally.

Chinese

opera

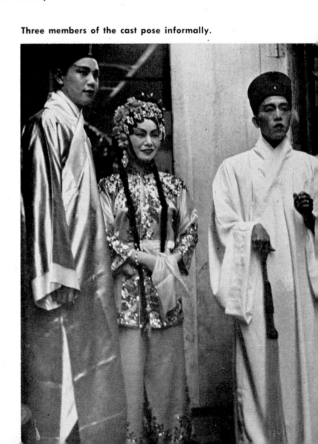

The cans of oil above are presented
by the Chinese to keep the
temple lamps burning.

Kwan Ti altar in the
Kong Chow Temple.

Objects on wall and lanterns
are offerings made at the
Kong Chow Temple.
Chairs in foreground are
richly embroidered.

51

The art of eating

*T*HE CHINESE WHOLESALE GROCER, smiling affably, said, "We eat and prepare all the Western dishes, and then," pointing around his establishment, "we also have all this."

Sacked, boxed or stacked, the unfamiliar ingredients of Chinese cuisine filled his warehouse—crinkly, heavy-headed white cabbage, dark green leaves of coriander, powdered green hide of ice melon, ginger root and water chestnuts. All but the chestnuts and ginger, imported from the Orient, were grown within 30 miles of San Francisco. "We tried once selling these things in Western-style grocery stores," said the wholesale grocer sadly, "but it didn't work out."

San Francisco's Chinese brought the ingredients of their cooking with them from the countryside around far Canton, and they planted their seeds around the bay. Their own menus, prepared in their own flimsy shacks, were far superior to anything that Gold Rush San Francisco had to offer and Chinese cooks were soon prized employees in the city's wealthier homes.

The Imperial dossier of Chinese recipes is said to contain 30 million different dishes. There are many who insist that Chinese cooking is the greatest in the world, an art developed through 40 centuries of painstaking attention. Among the varieties of Chinese cooking, one of the great styles is Cantonese, and that is the style of San Francisco's Chinatown. (Cantonese cooking does not include chop suey, which literally means "assorted little pieces," and is a fake imitation of Chinese cooking designed for Western palates.)

In China, it is a mark of caste to rise late in the morning —a sign that servants had taken care of the early morning chores. In San Francisco, where Chinatown is at its emptiest at 8 a.m., the day's first meal, when dining out, may well be

To the left, long Chinese
string beans. And below a
basket of dried squid.

Fresh snails.

taken at a tea house shortly before noon. The tea houses are characteristically open only from 10 a.m. to 3 p.m., and they are great centers of gathering and gossip for the wives of Chinatown's merchant princes.

The cuisine of the tea house contains, of course, tea, probably imported from Macao or Formosa. It also offers a rich variety of steamed things—fancy little delicacies which

Interior of Chinatown restaurant seen through octagonal window.

Westerners rarely see—cooked in bamboo baskets stacked one upon another from the steaming tray almost to the ceiling. The steamed dishes might include *jow fun jaw* (a meat-filled turnover with the outside made of taro root powder) or *ngow lay* (steamed tongue) or *ha gow* (a rice-flour wrapping around diced bamboo shoots and shrimp).

For the day's principal meal, in early evening, the diner will go to one of the great restaurants on or near Grant

Steamed food is prepared in
these bamboo baskets.

Chinese tomales or "tsung"
served during summer months.

Ginger root is a very popular
flavoring and ingredient.

Typical food served in a Chinese restaurant. Dishes contain:
Almond chicken, chow yuk, sweet and sour pork, prawns, won ton, fried rice.

Correct method of
chopstick holding.

Kitchen in world-famous Kan's restaurant.

Silver serving dishes
at Kan's hold fish,
Peking duck and lobster.

Fish market
with tank of
live fish in
window.

Avenue, all marvelously Cantonese except for a North China incursion of Peking Duck. The traveler will immediately notice that these restaurants seem to come in two types. Half a dozen of them are elaborate palaces of high cuisine, whose fame has extended throughout the Nation. Another dozen are less elaborate and less expensive but feature menus attractive enough to attract large numbers of Chinese and a few Caucasians who are "in the know."

The final meal of the day is a midnight bowl of rice gruel, fancier than the name sounds, which is eaten with sliced rice-flour crullers, a kind of Oriental doughnut, plus whatever else fancy dictates.

The Chinese are not notorious for drinking liquor in public, although they show a certain private fondness for their own *ng-ka-py*, a spirit distilled from herbs and said to be "of great potency." Chinatown's bars are recent additions to the scene and are populated more by tourists than inhabitants. The community's most popular beverage is of low potency, but it is not tea, as one might expect. It is good old American coffee.

Interior, grocery store.

Bar on Grant Avenue
laden with atmosphere.

Below, mosaic piano bar in the "Ricksha."

The best of two worlds

THOUSANDS OF PEOPLE jammed into Chinatown to witness the arrival of the Year of the Mouse. (It should have been termed the Year of the Rat, but the name was changed in deference to American tastes.) Days of festivities, punctuated by the staccato rattle of exploding firecrackers, climaxed in a night-time parade. Greeting the New Year, number 4658 on the Chinese calendar, was the final and most important performer in the parade, the block-long dragon carried on its swirling course down Grant Avenue by a total of 66 men.

New Year's Day is the biggest of Chinatown's many celebrations, a day when debts are paid, accounts settled and grudges forgotten. Like most of the festivals imported from China into San Francisco, it has no fixed date, but varies, like our Easter, with the state of the moon and the planets. For every Chinese, New Year's Day is his birthday, when he reckons himself to be one year older.

Fixed in date is the festival of Double Ten, the tenth day of the tenth month, when the dragon is again broken out to celebrate the Chinese Revolution and the collapse of the Manchu Empire, an event which began with a troop mutiny on October 10, 1911.

More sedate celebrations include the Moon Festival, a harvest time honoring of the autumn moon which takes place in September, and the Spring (or planting) Festival. The Winter Festival, celebrated entirely within the households with no public displays at all, has something of the flavor of Thanksgiving. The Ching Ming Festival is an annual outing to the graves in Colma, where the Chinese maintain private cemeteries. (Since the Communist Revolution, deceased Chinese are no longer reburied in the "sacred soil of China," as they formerly were in accordance with ancient

Various parade
participants and
group of lantern
girls below.

custom. San Francisco's Chinese are now buried in Colma, a suburb of San Francisco. Finally, Chinatown celebrates a number of festivals honoring various sages and deities, notably Confucius, the god of valor Quan Kung, and the gentle Quan Yin.

With all they brought with them from China, including their festivals, the older residents of Chinatown continue to live lives which are more Chinese than American. Unable to read English, they are avid consumers of one or more of the several local Chinese dailies. These papers, with national circulations up to 5000, are hand set in Chinese characters by printers who average five miles a day amidst their stand-up cases of type. Each paper stocks

Lantern girl and
musicians in
Double Ten parade.

Below, night view of famous block-long dragon, illuminated its full length.

around 5000 characters, and the printers have to know by memory where each one is pigeonholed.

The old people continue to patronize the herb doctor in the herb shop, although it is a sign of changing times that the number of Chinatown herb shops has dropped from 24 to six in the past ten years. (This is not entirely due to lack of patronage. The U. S. has a ban on imports from Communist China, which is the only source for certain of the herbs.) It is also a sign of changing times that a patient will ingest sea horse powder for a stomach ache and then, just to be on the safe side, proceed to see a Western doctor, who probably will be Chinese. Like the type for Chinese newspapers, the banks of small drawers in which the herbs are kept are unlabeled, and the herb dispenser must know where each concoction is kept by memory.

For the young people, the old ways are less important, and it is difficult to say how long Chinatown will remain a displaced fragment of the Orient. Insular at first by hostile necessity, Chinatown now goes its separate way for less compelling reasons—out of pride in its rich heritage and a determination not to lose this heritage entirely.

The New Year's parade passes.

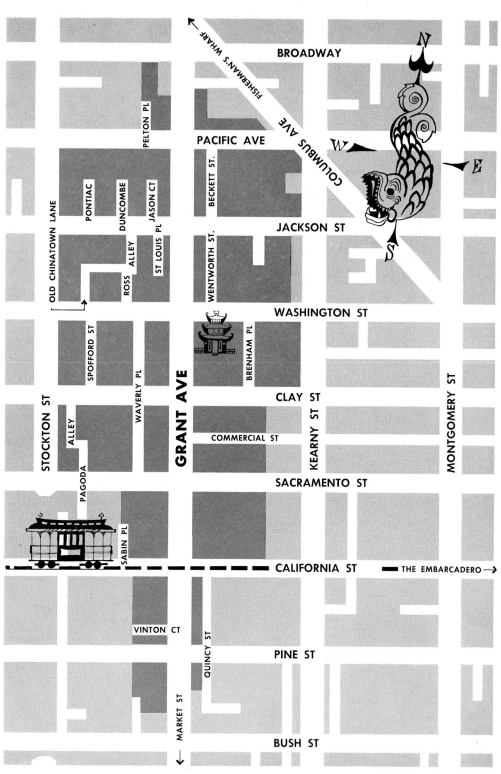

CHINATOWN, SAN FRANCISCO

Peking Duck

About the authors

This book is the result of a collaboration of photographer and writer who both find San Francisco a rich source for their work. This is one of several books on a San Francisco theme for the photographer, Phil Palmer. Jim Walls is a feature writer for the San Francisco *Chronicle* who for many years has been researching and writing on San Francisco subjects.

Phil Palmer

Jim Walls